# The Senses

# HEARING

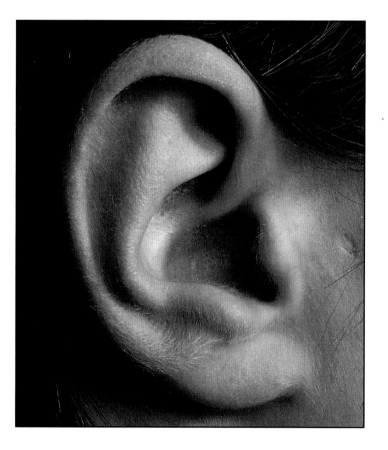

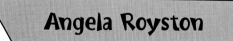

Angela Royston

Chrysalis Children's Books

First published in the UK in 2005 by
Chrysalis Children's Books
An imprint of Chrysalis Books Group Plc,
The Chrysalis Building, Bramley Road,
London W10 6SP

ISBN  1 84458 164 0

British Library Cataloguing in Publication Data
for this book is available from the British Library.

**Editorial Manager**  *Joyce Bentley*
**Senior Editor**  *Rasha Elsaeed*
**Editorial Assistant**  *Camilla Lloyd*

**Produced by Bender Richardson White**
**Project Editor**  *Lionel Bender*
**Designer**  *Ben White*
**Production**  *Kim Richardson*
**Picture Researcher**  *Cathy Stastny*
**Cover Make-up**  *Mike Pilley, Radius*

Printed in China

10 9 8 7 6 5 4 3 2 1

Words in **bold** can be found in New words on page 31.

Typography  *Natascha Frensch*
Read Regular, READ SMALLCAPS and Read Space; European Community Design Registration 2003
and Copyright © Natascha Frensch 2001-2004 Read Medium, **Read Black** and *Read Slanted*
Copyright © Natascha Frensch 2003-2004

READ™ is a revolutionary new typeface that will enchance children's understanding through clear, easily
recognisable character shapes. With its evenly spaced and carefully designed characters, READ™ will help
children at all stages to improve their literacy skills, and is ideal for young readers, reluctant readers and
especially children with dyslexia.

### Picture credits

Cover: Educationphotos.co.uk/Walmsley **Inside:** Bubbles: pages 6 (Lucy Tizard), 7 (Frans Rombout), 9 (Lucy Tizard),
12 (Frans Rombout), 13 (Pauline Cutler), 14 (Angela Hampton), 17 (Jennie Woodcock), 18 (Frans Rombout), 20 (Loisjoy
Thurstun), 22 (Frans Rombout), 24 (Loisjoy Thurstun), 26 (Angela Hampton), 27 (Loisjoy Thurstun), 29 (Loisjoy Thurstun).
Educationphotos.co.uk/Walmsley: pages 4, 11, 16, 21, 23. Steve Gorton: pages 1, 2, 5, 8, 10, 15, 19, 25, 28.

# Contents

# What is hearing?

Hearing is the **sense** that tells you about sounds and **noises** all around you.

Your ears and brain work together to give you your sense of hearing.

# Kinds of ears

Everyone's ears look slightly different on the outside. Ears can be many shapes and sizes.

Sounds go into each ear through the opening in the middle.

# Into your ears

The shape of your ears collects sounds, which then travel into your head.

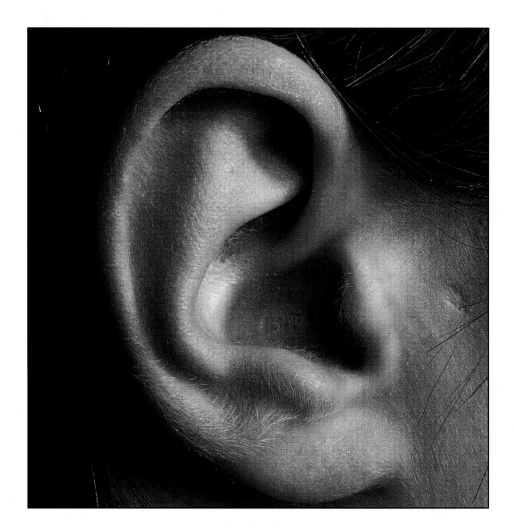

Putting a seashell or a cupped hand to your ear collects even more sounds.

# Loud sounds

Some sounds are very loud and clear. An aeroplane is very noisy.

Playing the drums or banging
with a hammer makes many
loud sounds.

# Quiet sounds

Falling rain can be quiet. Things sound quieter when you move away from them.

Whispering is talking quietly so no one else can hear.

# Even sounds

Hearing the gentle splash of waves on a beach makes you feel happy and relaxed.

The regular tick-tock sound of wind-up clocks and watches marks the passing of time.

# Musical sounds

Most people enjoy **music**.
Each kind of musical instrument
sounds different.

These children are making music. They are playing many kinds of instruments.

# Becoming louder

A **loudspeaker** makes quiet sounds louder. This CD player uses big loudspeakers.

**Headphones** and telephones have tiny loudspeakers inside them.

# Too loud

Loud sounds can hurt your ears. Covering your ears blocks out some of the noise.

Very loud noise damages your ears. This man wears special earmuffs to protect his ears.

# Deafness

Some people do not hear very well. They use a **hearing aid** to help them hear better.

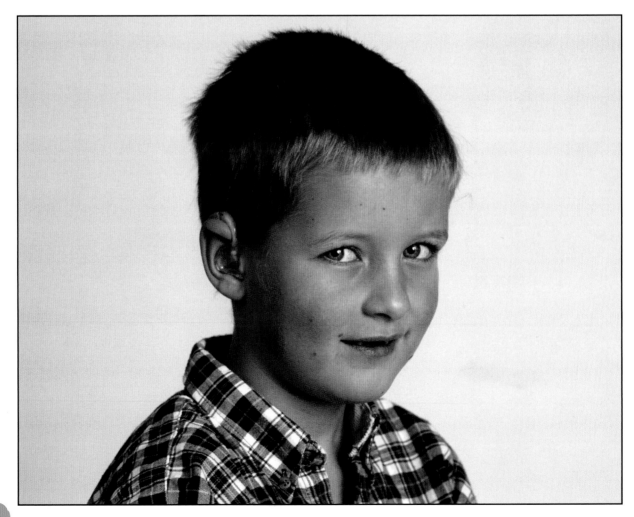

**Deaf** people can hear very little.
They use **sign language** to talk.

# Hearing well

To check your hearing, a doctor uses an instrument like this to look into your ears.

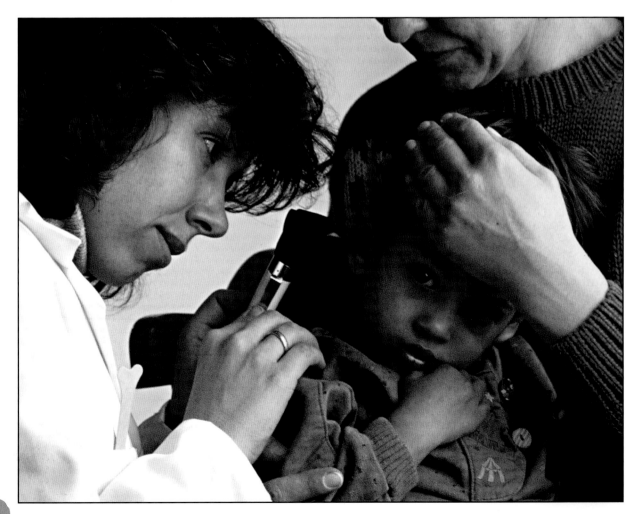

A **tuning fork** tests if you can hear a particular musical note.

# Ear infections

If you get an ear **infection**, you may find it hard to hear well.

A doctor checks your ears and gives you a special medicine to stop the infection.

# Ear care

When you wash your face, remember to wash the outside of your ears, too.

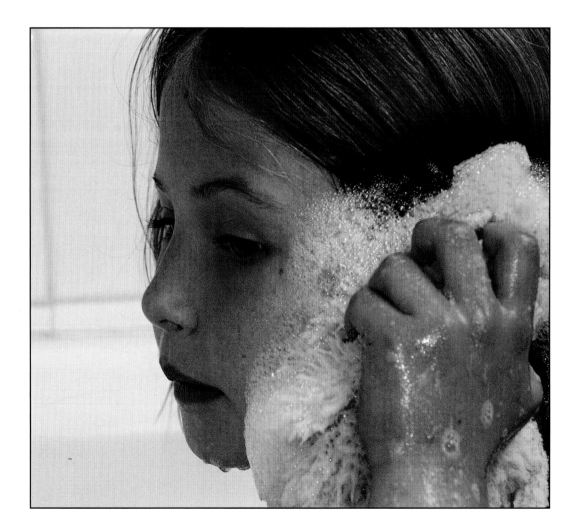

Dry your ears carefully when they are wet. Do not poke anything into your ear.

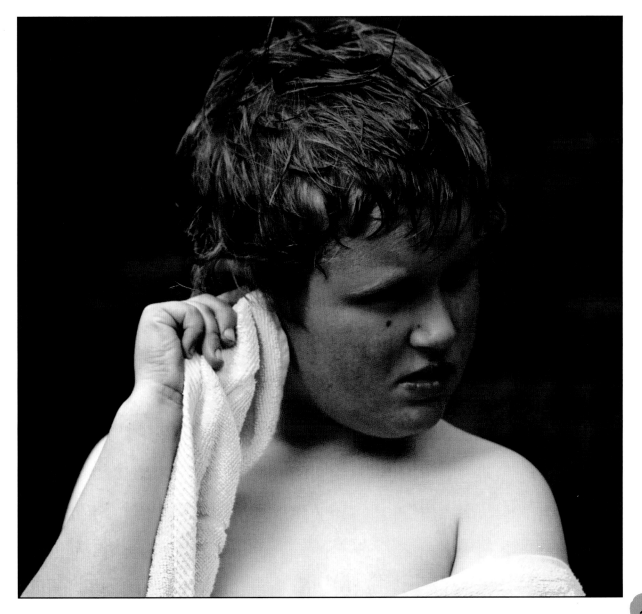

# Quiz

1 What can you do to help your ear collect even more sounds?

2 What kind of sound does beating a drum make?

3 Do things sound louder or quieter as you move away from them?

4 What is whispering?

5 What does a loudspeaker do?

6 Who uses sign language to talk?

7 What does a tuning fork do?

8 What makes an ear infection better?

The answers are all in this book!

# New words

**deaf**  unable to hear properly.

**headphones**  something that you put against your ears to hear sounds from small loudspeakers.

**hearing aid**  machine with a loudspeaker that helps people hear better.

**infection**  an illness that you catch.

**loudspeaker**  a machine that makes sounds louder.

**music**  a stream of sounds that sound pleasant.

**noise**  many different sounds at once.

**sense**  the way you find out about your surroundings. You have five senses – sight, hearing, smell, taste and touch.

**sign language**  using your fingers and hands to make signs that stand for words or letters.

**tuning fork**  an instrument that makes a pure musical note.

# Index